GHOST CHARACTERS

By the same author

Poetry

Overdrawn Account
This Other Life
Entertaining Fates
Lost and Found
About Time Too
Selected Poems
There are Avenues

Prose

Untitled Deeds

Translations

Selected Poems of Vittorio Sereni
The Great Friend and Other Translated Poems
The Greener Meadow: Selected Poems of Luciano Erba
Selected Poetry and Prose of Vittorio Sereni

Criticism

In the Circumstances: About Poems and Poets
Poetry, Poets, Readers: Making Things Happen
Twentieth Century Poetry: Selves and Situations

Editor

With All the Views: Collected Poems of Adrian Stokes
Liverpool Accents: Seven Poets and a City
Mairi MacInnes: A Tribute

PETER ROBINSON

GHOST CHARACTERS

for Katy
with love and thanks,
Peter
6 March 2006
in Cambridge

Shoestring Press

Typeset and printed by Q3 Print Project Management Ltd, Loughborough, Leics
(01509) 213456

Published by Shoestring Press
19 Devonshire Avenue, Beeston, Nottingham, NG9 1BS
Telephone: (0115) 925 1827
www.shoestringpress.co.uk

First published 2006
© Copyright: Peter Robinson
ISBN: 1 904886 25 6

Shoestring Press gratefully acknowledges financial assistance from Arts Council England

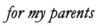

for my parents

Acknowledgements

Most of these poems first appeared in the following publications to whose editors grateful acknowledgement is made: *Agenda, BigCityLit, Cortland Review, English, Fire, fourW, Jacket, Kawauchi Review, Lynx, Matrix, Metre, New Grains, The North, nd [re]view, nthposition, Perihelion, PN Review, The Reader, The Sewanee Review, Shearsman, The Tanka Journal, Tears in the Fence, Times Literary Supplement,* and *Wandering Dog.*

A few were first published in Japan in a *hors de commerce* limited edition called *Anywhere You Like* (Pine Wave Press, 2000). 'Seasonal Greetings' appeared in the *Worple Press Catalogue 2002–3.* 'Facing Death' was selected for *In the criminal's cabinet: an nthposition anthology* ed. V. Stevenson and T. Swift (2004). The completed version of 'Untitled' was first printed in *Mairi MacInnes: A Tribute* (Shoestring Press, 2005).

Contents

ONE

UNPOPULAR SONG

Dropping through cloud toward rows of brick semis
where no one's to meet you, outstaying a welcome,
unpicked in the schoolyard, ill-favoured, revealing
you have been raped, have lied, or done time
starts that superfluous feeling.

Birdsong detached from the raucous dawn chorus,
tears before bedtime, a fit of the giggles,
needing a shoulder, sent to Coventry, stealing
home in the small hours: you know what it
means, that superfluous feeling.

Moroccans accosting fur-clad passersby
with a tray full of lighters, cassettes, razorblades;
loved names on gravestones; a drunk man reeling;
gooseberries, gijin, ones born every minute
get that superfluous feeling.

The fired, the jilted, left-handed or sad,
those given the push, erased from the photos,
untouchables, exorcised ghosts, those appealing
for clemency, justice, or just one more chance
sense that superfluous feeling.

The banter of beggars, buskers, soap-boxers,
and studying vacancies obviously bring it;
even survivors, the lucky, wounds healing
in thankfulness; even you, reader, have
had that superfluous feeling.

SEASONAL GREETINGS

1

At a blind-slatted window
in the Arts and Letters Building,
suddenly, thick snow
gusts, then starts to cling.

Through eyes grown weaker,
outside pales, as cold cure
powder clouds a beaker
of winter's imprisoning allure.

2

Look at them, fingers of an ornamental palm,
icy in surrounding mansion blocks' gloom.

Behind, a western-style bungalow winters
with clean drifts heaped around its door.

Flakes are gusting upward at each window,
another life gathering dust from years before.

JANUARY SALES

Drawn curtains show overnight snowfall
covering all with its blanket assurance;
but what looked like a fresh, clean start
is already pitted by the paper boy's prints,
and now comes news of futures market action.
Sunlight reflected off the piled-up snow
intensifies contrasts, adding a glow
to intent shoppers' faces that pass us by
wanting a marked down, end-of-line bargain.
They warily step on the treacherous ice,
a half-baked thaw just as suddenly refrozen;
and creatures thought to be extinct
stir in their frost as sleeping reason
breeds its cumbersome monsters once more.

At closing time, the sluggish moon's
risen above department stores;
but prices are jittery in further west time zones
as a few banks have had to close their doors.
Exchange rate graphs would zigzag like skiers;
there's panic buying in supermarket chains,
fast selling of stocks on the Bourse.
When frozen desires are melting like snow,
slush funds evaporate into the night,
names ruined, and promises to pay
the bearer written on flooded gutter water —
everything, everything must go.

CORNER STORE

Driving home one frozen night,
we were paused a moment
at an intersection's stop light;
like a fridge door left ajar,
up ahead, a corner storefront
window faintly glowed.

Late, and not a sign of life
disturbed the unfamiliar
business district, not one car
crossed while we were stationary;
no, but all these signs of lives
stencilled on wall-spaces had me
baffled how the shop survives
in extended shadow cast
by corporate finance offices.

Dispensing machines stood guard
beside the word *TOBACCO* —
and this corner retail outlet
stubbornly returned an echo
from the early modern past.
Its upper storey still had traces
of *CANADIAN PACIFIC*
outlined in patina'd dust ....

Stuck a while, we might have been
emigrants from some pestered shore
queuing outside to begin
ghost lives, our old ones gone awry
those minutes or long before
under just such a sky.

PAPER WORK

While our willowy daughter
with skirt in disarray
is lolling on the sofa
and fumbling with an imaginary cat
she dreamed was hers-to-keep once more,
talked of in her sleep last night,
her little sister's working at
a low wood table, scattered over
with grey card covered in scribbles,
colour swirls, cut-ups, collage
or folded origami paper —
all the signs of will and purpose
any fond parent might hope for.

Morning's flakes have blown away.
The girls, their cluttered interior,
are lit by winter sunlight —
a garden's sinuous branches
picked out with snow-filaments,
and shadows cast on frozen ground.
There have been tears, and will be smiles.

Meanwhile, at a loss to know
how this form's to be completed
(boxes filled out with a blood-group,
next of kin, phone numbers, faxes
in the event of human-made
and natural disaster: outbreak
of war, flash flood, or earthquake)
I keep an eye on them in hope
as they change and grow.

EXCHANGE VALUES

'Money is not only the medium of exchange, but
also a store of value, and the standard in terms of
which ... all kinds of relations between men are
more or less rigidly fixed.'

Piero Sraffa

1

Piero Sraffa, I remember,
came up to me once in Barclay's Bank.
'Young man,' he said, 'is that today's date'
— gesturing toward the blurred blank
of a wall — 'or the Interest Rate?'
I said: 'It's the thirteenth of September.'

2

But what could I say to those wealthy Japanese
tourists traipsing by my parents' house
off to photograph Paul McCartney's?
'Hello! Goodbye!' of course —
like the school kids do when I'm there
as they pass in their limousine bus,
wave, turn giggling heads to stare
at an alien, forgivably curious.

THE MONEY TREE

'*Nurse.* Is poverty a vice?
Lord B. Th' age counts it so.'
                        Ben Jonson

'Shake the money tree,' they say;
but I'd never seen one
until that Saturday in June
when at a temple garden
we came upon the gingko
(a pun in Japanese for *bank*)
with stacked-up one yen coins
fixed to the bark of its trunk ....
Little innocents, our daughters
had lined their apron pockets
with the weightless grey things
sight-seeing visitors stuff
in crevice, bole or crack
bringing some fortune, the luck
to be gifted with enough
for quarterly payments and debts.

As I helped to put coins back,
piled yen round its roots, or
balanced them in folds of bark
to fend off mortal shame
at finding you can't meet
employee pay or loan scheme,
it seemed the tree would choke
on so much token armour;
it seemed the time came back
when tempted with church offerings
I spent them at a sweet shop
and, found out, felt a shame,
a shame in genteel poverty's
scrimping, scraping, years of lack
as, pressed, dad would exclaim,
'Look, money doesn't grow on trees!'

THE LINES

'Non ti turbi il frastuono ...'
Vittorio Sereni

Over a pergola's gravel-dust shade
vine leaves quiver when expresses go by.
We're gathered for a goodbye party,
the last of many, our places laid;
and everyone's borne in mind.
                                    But you,
you're not even among the books upstairs
lining walls of a pensioned headmaster's
quiet room .... Now trains continue
not to disturb as they arrive or leave
with a clatter of closed shutters
on ochre frontage.
                         Seventy-six years
the house has echoed to a shunting locomotive,
coaches uncoupled through peace and war —
years absorbed by a blank façade
like absent presences of sounds heard
under the lines in a picture-hung interior,
non-ghosts, children who didn't come,
haunting them as you do, still, though
that fast train from sixty-odd years ago
has long since gone into their silent children's room.

USELESS LANDSCAPE

Now that houseplant shoots have hit the ceiling,
ivy bursts through parapet apertures
and pollen fluff seems to float on sullen air,
it must be time to take account
of thoroughfares pasted with false friends
or follow through habituated eyes
gaps between leaf clusters, how the land lies
athwart your expectations, loves, bad feeling.

With dusk and long distance concealing
children grown like a well-pruned rosebush,
months of everyday solitude
(nearer, nearer than the sound of blood
beating through one inner ear)
choke up the sources, run to seed, feeling.

By country club and golf course, unappealing
concrete towers return no echo —
not even clock digits staining them with rust;
repainted, white arrows at corners
gone round each weekday cannot recall
how anyone weathered those surfaces,
surfaces which won't weather themselves —
cast, enameled, fired to resist
any worn-smooth patches, patina, any feeling.

ABOVE THE FALLS

From a platform above the falls
half a gale's funnelling up through its gorge;
mountains are decked out in new leaves'
light green liveries, every one
given a buffeting like our hair
swept from foreheads by the same wind's force.

These tousled trees form a stadium wave,
fans' upraised arms, their noise
like the roar of allusions, rustling allusions
freshly re-amplified this year ....
Down through the busy valley, spume
of water cascading in a child's-eye-view
finds its power to exhilarate or scare
intact, still, sure.
                    But if I'm to represent them
they must have been elected too —
these examples of life's continuum,
yet in a more bracing air.

TYPHOON WEATHER

'Eh er singt und eh er aufhört,
Muß der Dichter leben'
Johann Wolfgang Goethe

'If this is life!' you said and sighed,
stumbling over a heap of shoes
one afternoon as we tried to leave —
the children fractious in all that noise.

*

Outside, on a ridge exposed
to every wind that blows,
branches, whole tormented trees
flailed like arms of women
fleeing a rape on some smoky canvas,
like the victim's upraised hands
in Goya's picture of reprisals —
as if the gale could be saying this,
or ripped leaves were expressive of it.

*

Fronds and debris through the air
were damage too; the pummelling rain
in gust-blasts buffeted our blue car —
while to roll under desperate boughs
struck me as uplift enough —
and how it has to be, if this is life.

NATURAL BEHAVIOUR

1

That's why entire arrays of things
through the hours' variable airs
are bullied by gusts, why evening's
natural colours in the storm-light and sun
take on intensities.
                        And it's as if repairs
were being made to our day —
as they are to a long wave of pine trees,
big IVF bags strapped round their bark;
and nature like a hospital's
all gesticulating twigs, blown blossom,
pointedly stretched-out petals ....

2

Now it's the turn of turquoise river sallows,
rose cloud, and leaf-tone in April.
Blue crows pause briefly on telegraph poles,
and a fire escape's guard-rail
is printed in shadow on a pale cream wall
expressing, expressing to the letter
how arrayed things may alter,
alter for the better, just before nightfall.

FACING DEATH

Death's a bit of a yob
who jostles you in the street;
staggering from some pub,
he has to pick a fight.

Past midnight, on hard shoulder,
you're running for dear life.
'Want to get any older?'
asks Death with gun or knife.

Perhaps he's a sorry loner,
or the guru of some cult;
still, you're dead and gone for
not pocketing an insult.

What is Death afraid of
that he needs to compensate?
Not seeming tough enough?
'Watch it,' says he. 'You wait!'

No, there's not much comical
about how we have to die;
perhaps for no reason at all,
for a look in the eye

or words I said, but twice ...
three times ... it's happened now.
Death's cuffed me in the face,
then turned and let me go.

GHOST CHARACTERS

for David Taylor

1

Then at the end of a long weekend
(a day of marriage celebrations,
container ships standing off between islands)
we went where lido restaurants'
wall-high windows opened
onto waves and a trampled beach;
vistas of the freshening breeze
hurried breakers towards that shore
and, though you'd think we were well out of reach,
some pursued us even here.

2

Ghost characters accosted us
in shadowy corners of late-night bars,
written out ghost characters
who can't remember what they've done,
never knew the harm they caused,
bringing back a time with them
when nettled, half-ashamed by words,
I left; but their compounded hurts
still stick to us like burrs.

3

Talk would exorcise them, clear the air,
taking with it such a one
as that drunk character driving home
who scared the living daylights from us
at earliest morning near the door
to another of life's safe houses.

4

There you stir in the midday haze
absorbed by an authentic wall
with stacks of stretched primed canvases,
a spare room possessed by nothing at all —
empty of ghosts like the bed's foot skeleton
waking a new woman up in her futon
from the 'former wife's return'.

5

From folds in the bedclothes they rise
with daylight, stubborn memories
of a misplaced past.

It's like glimpsing from a tour bus
stuck in traffic on some by-pass
people you have lost.

What do they come back for?
To deepen the morning? Make sure
you're alive at least?

6

Others badly done by, all the more
prone to spoiling acts
would knock the stuffing out of us.
Yet seeing as how, at last, pursuers
left for other haunts and these
misplaced persons were spirited away,
in a hotel lounge I breathed again;
the blocks of neon sprawl below
turned to scenes of habit, signs
of some relief.
                      But if content appears
and you've only competitive ears
to be heard by, how let anyone know?

7

Distanced, they come back again,
ventriloquized familiars
from circles of gossip or rumour,
as doing the different voices
you hint the one thing worse than being
talked about is being here.

Noh masks, devils' heads, bogeymen —
you're giving vent to all of these
and me, I'm mesmerized,
dazed, quite ready to believe
that talking makes it so.

8

This exercised them, filled the air
with spectres of those characters
that appear to go along with us
like running jokes or sores,
or like the coast road's ghost hotels'
ranked, reflective windows
overlooking an islanded horizon —
vast, abandoned structures
from which the trade had gone
away to Hawaii or to Guam.

9

No threat, they're almost missed ....
'The curse of a half-decent memory,'
you say, 'I'm repossessed by them.'
Yes, and so you promised
to drive me out that way some time;
we'd visit those vast, abandoned
structures from the past.

10

Walking out towards North Beach,
an angular coast of flat reclaimed land
in a Sunday blur brought back
the dome, apartments, far-fetched
landmarks, local habitats
overwhelmed with so much sky;
and I saw at last how grounds of habit
could alter the possible aired by
words — words letting us understand
they're not only what comes with the territory,
but what you do about it.

11

Now in the small streets, smells of drains
assail like mildness as passersby
bring to mind nobody else.
The currents form an ebb and flow
of diary entries, vanity mirrors,
dental floss, their *vitaes* of achievement
fading away with the sounding heels
under that expansive sky.

12

So, at the end of a long weekend,
we went where lido restaurants'
wall-high windows opened
onto freshening breeze and overcast skies
failing to cut the day down to size.

Gesticulating palm trees
made themselves felt like an offered hand
which stretched to include us in its grip,
each breath of the air kept up
by an ocean skyline's low release.

IN A FOG

Her father's death would mean the end. The dust sheets thrown on in Via Bixio, ghosts of chairs and tables freeze among air-roots of plants, heavy rustic sideboards, chill marble floors, old prints of the city, and her swirling abstract picture .... But now I've to leave them in his poor corner, hunched up on the bed perhaps, around them typescripts, scrawls, turned pages, chess men, dictionaries, and the fierce cold. They would be talking quietly. Her whole world, which had seemed much more secure than his, was suddenly falling to pieces. Her father, by means of a promissory note, had sunk the family fortune in another's bankruptcy. He'd been ruined by a lifelong friend.

So what was this friend of mine trying to do? He would help her through the perishing season, help her over an unspoken wound. Yet at the funeral, he was just an interloper. They'll accuse him of only wanting her money, her inheritance. Inheritance? The family was putting what properties remained in different names, to save the little left, though even the lawyers — as it transpired — were picking clean their bones.

Now I'm in that icy damp, nose streaming on the Ponte Catena. Fog's so dense both San Zeno and Borgo Trento have disappeared. There's just this greyness everywhere. A blurry orange glow before me — Renon's ice cream sign — is the only kind of reassurance .... Her people are like frozen statues in the park back there: the relations between them obscure, the *dramatis personae* a muddle of names. Yet dear among them is his blonde Italian, with a butterfly grip in her drawn-back hair. She'll be sat beside him on that rumpled bed. He'll have his arm around her shoulder. He's trying to talk himself back into her life.

TWO

OUT OF HARM

There's a weight on my eyelids tonight
like pennies from somewhere, two coins,
the late light glowing like
that sliver of a moon born yesterday.

I'm going to sleep, but not quite yet.
It's your death weighs them down,
your death as inexplicably
fact as the bare fact of that moon.

More, later dream light brings back
even your horrified husband
to whom I would offer condolence;
but he can't take it, and disappears.

Which leaves me in an early dawn
still wondering what it was happened
to you, you really a ghost,
a ghost from those first years,

what drove you to such an idea,
to do yourself in like Father Time
but leave us hanging, hanging on
here with our questions which weigh

like the weight on my eyelids last night,
those pennies from somewhere, two coins,
and the late light glowing like
that sliver of a moon born yesterday?

BEYOND RECALL

Now winter, the land gone monochrome,
winter turns to us with trees
wind's blown holes through; distances
slip back like burrowing memories,
the snowflakes melted as they fall.

Again there's a grey in the atmosphere's
car fumes, snow, and as it happens
chilly, stung, burning ears
need words breathed beyond recall,
a sense made from that final act.

Because you went against the ears
of parents, mentors, friends,
again — come a grey in the atmosphere's
drizzling snow — it's as if you'd gone on
but without us, having killed us all.

The air-starved blood stopped in your veins.

GOING NOWHERE

The fairground's wire fences
are impacted with blown snow;
and with traffic at a standstill,
glass steamed up, we're here
like our own dead who stay
in their frozen ground,
old thoughts, or just thin air.

They've not melted away,
have not passed beyond,
crossed border or frontier
and even when blown snow
impacted on mesh fences
vanishes, they don't go.

COME TO GRIEF

Those hills of the eastern skyline
are a shrouded corpse in late dawn mist,
a corpse outleant —
no, not the year's, the century's, two millennia's,
I'm dreaming this because it's yours,
here once more at breakfast time
with one more dawn above those hills;
and my daughter, seeing them,
comments on brave watery sunshine
glistening in rivulets
over rooftops, plate-glass windows,
down to the riverbanks' first cars,
to kiosks, shrines, convenience stores ...
and now she says she wants to draw its
whole array, and that's a promise.

With all this newness, how my daughter
gazes at the world you left,
at the Kamo's murky water
flowing away, where a faint sun glints,
flowing like promises come to grief;
and dreaming this because it's yours,
that shrouded corpse in late dawn mist,
I ask myself what will support her, at least,
in its disappointments.

THE GIST OF IT

Down Kawabatadori
a line of weeping willows
in chilly dawn's diffused sunlight
droops over the Kamo; white heron,
squadroned for their fly-past,
skim that skin of water.

The willows find you strayed
in a novel of sensation
and shiver at the bits of story,
shiver at how you tried
to protect your reputation
threatening suicide.

Too proud! Too proud, they said,
you wouldn't take the loss
of self-esteem, bought land,
a home you'd planned to build,
the loss of house, of status
or family lying down.

                    *

Now snow lies dusted on chilled earth
traced with criss-cross footprints —
and then a memory in this light
returns with how you told
of ruined executives desperate enough
to leap off Kiyomizu temple's
platform on that hillside —
any where, any where out of the world!

So driven to extremity
yourself by threat and counter-threat
you took it out on all of us,
on another life in your womb:

another life you couldn't let
catch its breath; it starved with you
for want of what the heart wants ....

Under strings of New Year lanterns
gleaming red and white
at entryways of late night bars,
cars' rear- and headlight beams
bring back a sunrise at Tsu beach,
two 'watchers of the trickling gore'
dying 'waves that lapped the shore'
exactly a decade ago.

Poor shadow, now I know
at least the gist of it
and in this cold dawn light
would fathom how someone I taught,
someone who taught me 'See you later',
taught me 'Anywhere you like'
or how to ask for a glass of water,
would be driven to that extremity —

your long game pulled up short.

MONTHS GONE

The pine trees stand their ground
and form a rolling wave as
up the slope blows chilly wind:
this season doesn't love us.

Months gone, you seem long dead
at a crime scene with no body —
as if the solid world had
forgotten you already.

Its camellias are frost-blighted
in a silence not of love;
but love of life, though unrequited,
is the only one we have.

SURFACES OF THINGS

Surrounded by crows
near the writers' museum,
a child threw her crumbs.

Grass tufts had thrust through
asphalt to the castle grounds'
abandoned classrooms.

Currents on the lake
drew a pink line of blossom
across poised water.

Then fresh breeze ruffled
trim feathers on a hawk's wings:
surfaces of things.

That's what it felt like.
A scattering of dark leaves
stood up, chased tourists,
chased till the wind dispersed them —

embittered posthumous lives.

THE SILENCES

So why else notice
a girl in black pass by,
and how she's lifted
on heels some inches nearer
a clear late afternoon sky?

*

Your tiny maisonette
with precipitous staircase
stays closed up, unsold
and unsellable because
a suicide was in it.

*

Whispers on the phone
accuse you of selfishness,
a scapegoat victim
to exonerate the living.
They allow you all the blame.

*

This party's silence —
now each of those who knew you
won't even mention
your sudden non-existence:
it's as if they didn't know.

*

Here the custom is
not even to utter the word.
So, after all these
years and years you're teaching me
still, post-mortem, Japanese.

NOT ON YOUR LIFE

Spring rain falling and droplets on my lenses
smudge the things' margins;
there's a reddish blur in branches just before
blossom bursts as pink-white floss.

On soggy ground, pine needle rafts
are washed up at corners of gutters or curbs.
How avid earth absorbs
all a sullen sky can hurl at it, and more!

I'm not saying there might have been more
to make of pale green catkins
or tardy blossom battered by rain,
then lost far too fast this miserable year.

Only look at how distance is shaded away
in ground-level clouds and the mist,
how fun fair flags droop in a lack of any wind,
boughs hang heavy with what petals remain.

And though you were more or less blind
not wearing your glasses, I'm lost
as to why the phenomenal world
should come to seem so terminally vain.

Then let's say I'm the one mistaking
my revived self for this spring day —
although it's as if your brittle life passed
like all the four seasons in a single day.

Let's say no one's denying you the right
to end it all by killing time,
end the palaver, a dull sun's gleam,
these buds and leaves that require you here ....

Oh have it your own way.

MORE BORROWED SCENERY

'But her sense I had misunderstood
imagining friendship ...'

Climbing the road home's snaky curves,
I catch earth's rim, its margin hazed,
this dusk gilt-edging cloud wisps
trailed beyond a tree-fringe, frayed;
yet can't for the life of me see
how you could feel so dead to the world,
or let the world feel dead to you.

Still in lacking light you'll never say,
but beckon me out of life's ruin
as if to salvage whatever you can,
and not be put off by silence
from someone deciding to take his bat home,
no, not over your dead body —
though over your dead body it would be.

LENGTHENED SHADOW

Footpath grasses glinting with rain
by a pungent creosoted fence
are well-found first solidities
where, recessed into wooded hillside,
dark waters, still, a remnant of moat
glistening through the day provide
their plain antidote.
                            These scents
of almond and crab-apple blossom
mingled with, then overwhelmed
by creosote on fencing bring
home how much, not here,
you cast a lengthened shadow
over this springtime's
changing light, its cloud forms;
yes, you cast a lengthened shadow,
one I can't step out of.
                            Now
from buds and petalled branches,
a fluting thrush descants
on the chit-chat of tits or finches.
Taking a hint from that chorus,
spirits rise in sheets as dawn
flares condensation-beaded panes.
Still only a lost acquaintance,
it's as if you haunted them or me —
as if shadowed I ought to find myself
in love, in love with your memory.

THREE

A CONSTITUTIONAL

for Teresa Mutalipassi

There's breeze along the promenade,
enough to stir some pendant leafage
over-fringing the broad water side
ringed with rain, a storm's presage.

Yet even this turn in the season
leaves me unruffled: whatever's wrong
isn't likely to be weather then;
now cloud comes rumbling headlong.

Feeling foreign everywhere,
just as the Kursaal convalescents
try to recover a sense of life's presence,
I pause beside the lake and stare.

PARMESE DAYS

It comes to this anonymous tree,
pollarded, with thin leafed branches
pushing out at fiercer angles
from its remnant stumps gone grey:
you're here each morning at the glass,
the kitchen door, a roo-coo of doves
and brick end-wall for scenery.

Those violet-grey doves flutter
up through the vine leaves
trailed along a green mesh fence,
a line of barbed wire on its top;
daily this happens, and a stray cat
limps by on three legs, as chance
would have it, without a drop
of aura or memory or even sense
now I know you better.

Notice, at the tree trunk's base,
how one plastic garden chair
has not been sat on for some time.
That upturned bath, the building gear
and you are grown familiar —
breeding dismay, like bare facts
or as if this view from a kitchen window
were all the panorama left here —

which I cling to, nonetheless,
while sunlight starts to settle me;
the August stillness has its day;
another round of ripening grapes,
green chestnuts is upon us, still,
in a literal Italy.

IMPOSSIBILIA

'He saw an immense prospect; it went; and the world was as before.'
Thomas Hardy

Low on the horizon, as we drove,
sheet-lightning flared through cloud-cover
and, arriving, broke in great rain splotches ....

Sheltered where the old world was still stored,
we were repairing from life's main force
among poor daubs, musty tomes, and the worse
furniture, pieces to be restored.

                    *

That August thunder, or what I thought rain,
pummelled on a roof's defective skylights;

but battering at them, hail's ice-pellets
pattered across cracked varnish and veneer.

Although the heavens would press their point here,
none of those objects tickled your palates.

                    *

Another time, summer lightning started
in forks or broad flashes instantly to show
immense prospects: insistently, a city's
complexes came and went with loud reports.

Down by a terrace French window fixed open
against oppressive heat, the night sky,
you lay still fathoming how changes happen
seeing as it's not too late to try.

THE RED CLOUD

'What is it?' 'A cloud, a red cloud ...'
— and with her words I saw one
above a seaport skyline
of house façades, church frontages,
tenements, wharves and jetties
flattened, lit up like a stage set
by the setting sun.   A red cloud,
two shades, smudged at the edges
had interposed itself between
us and a burning disc dropped down,
painting the town red as it went
behind slates, aerials, chimney pots —
its aureole lingering with us still
though the source had gone.
                                          Clear
of the strait our ship was headed
across a gulf, an offing freaked
with fiery dashes. On its fore-deck
passengers were craning necks back
towards remains of an English seaman
put ashore with fever, who
lies buried high above the town.
(You look out from his cypress shade
to where that burning disc will drown
in a sea horizon).
                              This red cloud
scorched by rays at their most intense
moments before sun disappears,
this lets you understand
our day has had it, it's finished
now the ferry pitches homeward
into night, night's possible outcomes,
once these fireworks are done.

POSTHUMOUS SEASIDE

'il poco di oro che rimane
sulle piccole isole
postume al giorno tra le scogliere in ombra'
Vittorio Sereni

1

What with the flashes of white moored yachts
crowding Bocca di Magra's marina,
turbulent water, fauna on the sea,
as we reach here in sunlight and car fumes
it's difficult not to remember
those two climbing that far hill one April
at the start of the Falklands-Malvinas business,
their quarrels effaced in a later air;
it's difficult not to recall
the others who, since they liked it here,
remain in their uncertainty
waiting at jetty or pier.

2

With traces all but passed away,
we come through a pine wood
then one of beach umbrellas
here with our three-year-old
perched up on shoulders,
and the murmur of lost words
through a palisade swells;

we see Fiumaretta's bay
curving from marble-slab mole
round to Massa and Carrara, see
the swimmers tread water
or strike back towards
alluvial sand, a gritty grey.

41

3

And grey the pill-box still on its cliff face
is flaky, graffitied with slogans,
evaporated memories
now world or cold war warriors are gone
leaving behind old soldiers' tales
retold for their sakes like reprisals,
us fated to be custodians
for memories not our own.

4

From lost Septembers, now what dies
is nostalgia for a past not mine
on final beaches of this year —
ones you'd barely recognize.

There's not much beach left either:
more gnawed by winter storms,
what's left roped off for those who live
renting umbrellas and deck chairs.

Yes, you'd barely recognize
the sewage pounded by high waves,
or summer rubbish tide-line
with its haunting flies.

5

Then there'd have to be smoke-plumes
in palls spread over mountains,
diaphanous, from forest fires
turning slopes to patches
of scorched earth like last-gasp desires
to assume the world that parents saw
post-war —
illusory hopes among burnt remnants,
become ashes and light in the air.

6

We're wading through breakers to reach
the cove of Punta Corvo,
this Sunday afternoon's last beach —
and here come the people from Parma,
Milano, Carrara, who-knows-where ....
Among them, another poor swimmer
invaded by the sea's strength,
custodian of revenants' memories
far removed from pasts not his
stands gazing at the tide-line.

Lucky to be spared those years,
he hears in the strength of the sea
voices recounting mistakes
through this season or lost ones to save us,
sun like lightning on each wave
and in the last boats' wakes.

7

So take one final summer swim,
be tumbled in the surf
and find thoughts turn to him or him
or others nowhere more alive
than in among the topless bathers,
their tanned, leathery hide
under a mute September sun
to all the world pre-mummified,
as if readying themselves for oblivion.

ALL UNAWARES

Packed clouds, away above cypresses,
bring back disappointments
in a washed-out holiday's end.
It seems you've missed one more of the chances
for being changed and, yes, your life's
about to be returned
to the season's happenstances,
more than possible, the safe
or sorry .... Yet something in this air
still promises a warm spell broken,
great change come to their heat-stunned plain.

Perhaps that smell's the chlorophyll
released from greenery in need of a rinsing
mingled, perhaps, with dust stuck down
now earth lies dissolved by rain.

Our summer, it seems, has found an end
in the cracking of a branch outside
and splintered boughs tormented
by a storm's incessant wind.

Yes, it seems the newly-charged, the scented
atmosphere itself has changed your mind.

OPERA SEASON

Drum rolls, trumpets, explosions of light
came closer beyond our talk as talk
turned to the chorus of Hebrew slaves
losing their balance on a wobbly set
where Babylon's towers might refuse to crack
or, given the Arena's size,
a *prima donna* couldn't simply blink her eyes ...
when suddenly, as if by way of illustration,
the young singer-understudy at our table
darted a look round, turning her whole head
with melodramatic surprise.

The restaurant awning hung heavy with rain.
With tumult, stage-lit, the heavens had opened
over Verona and early enough
to cancel that evening's *Aida* —
time enough, though, for the tenor's return
as he wound us up with his recitative:
spoiled love plots taking place against a drop
of foreign affairs, dead bottles, empty plates,
ghost characters' words, resentments, despairs
tumbling into air every-which-way
like an echo of the storm outside.

There were so many things he needed to say.
Begging to differ in a brief duet
she hoisted the tension near breaking point.
Like it or not, at that climax our table
sat frozen in a tableau for finale and curtain —
the rained-off evening now a washed-out night
to be aquaplaning the long road home.
Holding the audience still in their sway,
suddenly tension drained out of this scene
for all we could hear on our rickety set
was a creaking from the tomb.

ELECTRIC STORM

for Anthea Robinson

You love its sound on a canvas awning,
a caravan roof or car's —
or on this house, some people dining
by candlelight with ancestors
flash-lit along the walls, remaining
inside life's shadowiness, as was,
and the standby illumination shining
mildly on faces, children's,
till power's restored like the dawning
of an aspect, a family resemblance,
here, where it isn't always raining.

PERPETUAL ELSEWHERE

Yet darkening, closing with short words
in kiosk, bar, dry-cleaning outlet
routine's features can't but tell
how your face now doesn't fit
and the sense you shouldn't be here,
have overstayed the season's welcome,
litters chestnut boulevards —
their diseased leaves bidding us farewell!

Forgive me, yet again,
if I don't have a good word for them,
seem to have fallen out of love
with leaf-strewn avenues after rain,
with Arcadian temple and football team;
these are the terms of disengagement,
given this broadest hint from autumn
and, besides, it's time we went.

TSUKIHAMA

for David Gilbey

1

Early after the typhoon passed
on a beach awash with driftwood,
shell pieces, debris, and wrack,
we got by flooded tide-pools
and, stranded, waited for the news
of pleasure cruise schedules —
though there'd be nothing all day,
what with the still high seas,
narrow channels, and stiffening breeze.

2

That's why we'd have to make do
with a fisherman baiting his line,
wind gust and inrush of waves
letting our two girls play.

Curious, how they gain a taste
for fragments of furniture, say,
ones worked by all four elements,
burn marks smoothed in their grain.

3

But nobody needed to tell them
of the sea's unforgiving floor
as they hung on our legs in the foam.
Instinctively they knew its power,
its breaking swell and undertow.
That same power you brought home
telling of an Australian PM
gone missing on his daily swim —
his very important person never found.

4

No sign of moon in broad daylight
unless the crescent-like curve of beach
had given this place its name —
and given a name to its array
of jostled boats moored down a mole
built out in concrete along the low headland;
at intervals, the next bay's spume
would spray through its wind-bent pines.

5

It was here in the general neglect
house doors opened on a still silent alley;
here we reversed past anchor heaps
rusting in a house-end's deeper shadow,
found rose-blooms of nets on the sea wall
and ornamental palm trees' hairy bark
with, speckled about each trunk,
pink-flowered mesembryanthemum.

It was here, despite a biker's roar,
here that casual clutter and the rest
of the place's life seemed set to resist
erosion and encroachment all around.

6

Yes, it seemed as if resentment
had been burned off by the sunlight,
as if not a shadow of regret
clung to this bather striding from shallows,
his torso wreathed in kelp —
or else to this gleaner of seaweed
who kept hauling fronds from the tide
and heaped them there in warm sand,
as if helping tidy up the world.

SURFACE TENSION

Wave Island, my equivocal isle,
etched in the pellucid air;
Wave Island with its pine-tree profile,
a skein of water peeling off there
on the low horizon;
white lighthouse at the seaboard side,
its few outlying rocks
hardly lathered in a minimal tide
this autumn afternoon: it looks
flatly tranquilized —
what with the offing like a vast lake
forming sheets of reflections
ruffled by pleasure craft or us as we break
that stillness and find our actions
baffle being out of season ....
So we had broken the skin of it
swimming out part way
into the calm and I have to admit
Wave Island from this fisherman's bay,
it didn't look the same
as we floated on the Pacific Ocean
seeing dragonflies mate in mid-air;
and while they skimmed its surface tension,
my equivocal isle of just last year
turned a benign, enigmatic face towards here.

THE FLOW

Dead tired, day standing at the windows,
in a haze of wakefulness, pretend
there's nothing else for it but to lie
with life's gifts or misgivings, with sounds,
the children's voices inhabiting air
for a moment, to fade at the next alley corner.
That's how morning comes and goes.

At twelve, I get up to open a window.
Some rainfall dimples the surface
of a slow-shifting river's perpetual flow,
each ripple like visible time, a fever
searching through joints and sinews.
It's low tide: disused mooring blocks
lie revealed in all their slime.

Like tears that speckle car windscreens
after they're parked out under pines,
water-drops form across canvas
shop awnings, trickle into a flow
of thoughts, being barely awake,
thoughts of the famous town skyline
with neon switched off in the small hours,
ghost characters just before dawn
hardly recalled by the current below ....

The water-drops teeter, glint and go;
and all this blurs on the edge of sleep
to leave with practically nothing, nothing,
nothing that will not keep.

AGAINST HIMSELF

This double exposure in black and white is
Uncle Bobby playing chess.
It's as if the two sides of his face
were competing people, though their ties'
identical knots give them away.
The him on the right's just pushed a piece
and now he sits with supercilious
look for ever fixed on half that face.

The other's in quite a quandary, a trap.
Though he holds his chin like Rodin's *Thinker*
playing up the differences
between his mirrored self and one opponent,
he's caught, can never finesse an escape.
Besides you know his weaknesses of old;
ah yes, but then he knows yours.
Study more carefully the positions —
White's a piece up, yet Black has past pawns;
both kings alone and almost mated,
neither has anything like sound defences.
So there we are: the self-defeated.

'Not at all,' says he, 'I don't even have to choose
whether I'm going to win, or when I lose.'

POINT OF VIEW

Face it, at waking, the view
from a spare bedroom window
is of sparse pasture, a hedge or two,
blanched, but not in snow —

sky cross-hatched by the branches' vein-work,
everywhere rimed with frozen fog,
that line of grimy cars
abandoned like whited sepulchres ....

Though driven back onto your own devices
as if it were all taking place in the head,
just see for yourself things as they are —
which is the point of you.

ALONG THESE LINES

1

Iced-over, the wharves flare in sunshine.
Frost sticks on grass tufts; snow-melt's refrozen.
A church clock shows just ten past nine.

Like the rare half-timbered house fronts,
blanketed hills form a monochrome scene
from tree, stone wall, and occasional roof line.

2

This scene gives way to green mildew on cuttings
hewn out of the Pennine chain;
and you sense once more how heart-strings
were drawn taut along these lines —

lines that had taken us up to mum's family,
taken me over to college
then home again with a degree.

3

Crisp autumn leaves lie among red ferns
even now, swathes of low-hanging rain cloud
cut with blue splotches and light,
with cumulus auras or raking beams.

A twig in its mouth, that up-started crow
brings back rebukes to me, back
from Garforth's church with its clock
stopped now thirty-two years ago.

4

Through early mist a brazier's
burning pallets in its wrecker's yard.
Between the silver-birch saplings
suddenly black and white magpies take flight;
and it's as if the strings
of your heart, drawn taut across it,
have found their way through the litter of years.

5

Derelict mills are still on valley floors
by winding river, over straighter canal
and flights of outstretched lock-gate arms.

6

Yet as the farmed fields rise to moor pasture
there's a thinning of the signs
like winter trees seen on a skyline's
turning curve, its mausoleum
of ash-grey cloud heaped up behind them ...

Never mind, you must manage the remainder.

UNTITLED

'absolute circumstance'
Mairi MacInnes

Invited to take
a last train back from the park lake,
I take a long look at its waves
stiffly glinting through thick leaves.

The track between an avenue's oaks
rattles off from that water-side
refreshment chalet veranda and makes
passing vistas cut us down the ride.

There are style marks on the landscape's
contours, garden deities
with orifices flaked like chapped lips
stood petrified among the trees.

Reflections in carriage panes have me
trying to resist the given: far
dusks that tinge days in this country,
such things being what they are ....

*

Two girls emerge from a maze's hedge;
then we lead them by the hand
round that ornamental fountain edge,
its water fogged with weed and slime.

Yet it holds pink clouds in transit,
lank fronds clinging under them;
the girls step out as if past time
were no more than a stagnant pond,
balancing precariously on its rim!

*

Roped-in once more for an evening service
at the house chapel, I knelt in prayer
like when, however many years before,
you stared into the dark of closed eyes
still in time and let them pass —
those moments each containing all there is
by way of punishments or bliss.

*

Back then, I picked up from cut lawn
a moulted feather and let the wind
lift it wherever —

over these frontages, gardens and pond
with there, at no distance, a park lake
looking like the next to last of England.

OCCASIONAL SUNSET

Closing curtains on an opened-up sky
you pause to let change happen
in its own time or while
crows wheel about like bits of night,
the turquoise vault's empurpled,
pink-flecked, become lurid violet.

Lower, leaf cluster and grass pile
turn viridian from emerald
in the falling night which follows
like a threat or cadence
swelling time gone as work-filled blurs
now to a green after-light.

So even the worst days were ended
leaving us to figure out the dark —
how it's not what anybody intended,
but this come by default that says
we were alive to our lives
when it was one of those days.

Notes

Unpopular Song: 'gaijin' is the shortened form of 'gaikokujin' and means the equivalent of 'foreigner' in Japanese.

Exchange Values: the epigraph is from Piero Sraffa's 'Dr Hayek on Money and Capital', *Economic Journal*, vol. XLII, March 1932, p.43. I'm grateful to Peter Edwards for prompting the memory and so the poem by showing it to me.

The Money Tree: the epigraph is from Ben Jonson, *The New Inn*, V.i. 56-7. The fact that 'gingko' is a homophone with the Japanese word for 'bank' may not necessarily be the reason why these trees are sometimes festooned with small coins.

The Lines: the epigraph, meaning 'Be untroubled by the roar', is from Sereni's 'A M. L. sorvolando in rapido la sua città', addressed to his future wife who was from the Parma area.

Useless Landscape: the title was suggested by a song of Antonio Carlos Jobim's called 'Inutil Paisagem'.

Typhoon Weather: the epigraph, meaning 'Before he sings and before he ends, / The poet must live', is from Goethe's 'Dreistigkeit' in the *West-östlicher Divan*. The Goya painting is, of course, his 'Le Tres de Mayo 1808'.

Ghost Characters: The 'former wife's return' is a print by Shun'ei and Sunshō Katsukawa from a book of ghost stories called *Imawa-mukashi* (1790). There is a copy in the British Museum. My poem is set in Fukuoka.

Out of Harm: 'Father Time' is the character in Thomas Hardy's *Jude the Obscure* who hangs himself and his siblings 'because we are too menny' in chapter two of part six.

Come to Grief: the phrase 'a corpse outleant' is from Hardy's 'The Darkling Thush'. The Kamo is the river that flows through Kyoto.

The Gist of It: Kawabatadori is a street running along the eastern side of the Kamo River. Kiyomizu dera is one of Kyoto's most famous temples, built on a high platform supported by wooden stilts. The penultimate verse cites my own 'At New Year' in *Lost and Found* (1997).

More Borrowed Scenery: the epigraph is taken from my 'In the Borrowed Scenery', also in *Lost and Found*.

Impossibilia: the epigraph comes from Hardy's 1882 novel *Two on a Tower*.

Posthumous Seaside: the epigraph, meaning 'the little gold light remaining / on the tiny islands / posthumous to the day between already shadowed rocks', is from 'Un posto di vacanza', Sereni's long poem set at Bocca di Magra, where many writers and artists would, and some still do, spend their summer vacations.

Electric Storm: 'the dawning of an aspect' and 'a family resemblance' are formulations that appear in Wittgenstein's later philosophy.

Tsukihama: the poem is set in Okumatsushima, a little further north along the Pacific coast of Miyagi prefecture from the more famous Matsushima. 'Tsuki' means 'moon' and 'hama' means 'beach' in Japanese.

Surface Tension: this poem is also set at Tsukihama and alludes to my 'Equivocal Isle' in the last section of *Selected Poems* (2003).

Along these Lines: the lines in question are those from Liverpool Lime Street to York Station. Garforth is a village just east of Leeds — where the Rachel who appears in 'Scargill House' from *About Time Too* (2001) lived at the parsonage.

Untitled: the epigraph is from Mairi MacInnes's poem 'Morning on the Estuary, Noon at Sea' in *The Pebble: Old and New Poems* (2000). My poem is set at Castle Howard in Yorkshire. The last line naturally refers to Ford Madox Brown's 'The Last of England' — a painting of emigrants.

OTHER BOOKS FROM SHOESTRING PRESS

HALF WAY TO MADRID: POEMS Nadine Brummer. *Poetry Book Society Recommendation.*
ISBN 1 899549 70 6   £7.50

BROXTOWE BOY: A MEMOIR Derrick Buttress. ISBN 1 899549 98 6   £8.95

MY LIFE AS A MINOR CHARACTER Derrick Buttress. ISBN 1 904886 16 7   £8.95

BLACK RAINBOW: a novel by Philip Callow. ISBN 1 899549 33 1   £6.99

PASTORAL Philip Callow. ISBN 1 1904886 06 X   £8.95

TESTIMONIES: NEW AND SELECTED POEMS Philip Callow. With Introduction by Stanley Middleton. A generous selection which brings together work from all periods of the career of this acclaimed novelist, poet and biographer. ISBN 1 899549 44 7   £8.95

TARO FAIR Ian Caws. ISBN 1 899549 80 3   £7.50

THE GOODBYE EDITION Carole Coates. ISBN 1 904886 18 3   £8.95

THE WEIGHT OF COWS Mandy Coe. ISBN 1 899549 97 8   £7.95

INSIDE OUTSIDE: NEW AND SELECTED POEMS Barry Cole.
ISBN 1 899549 11 0   £6.95

GHOSTS ARE PEOPLE TOO Barry Cole. ISBN 1 899549 93 5   £6.00

THE CARTOGRAPHER SLEEPS Barbara Daniels. ISBN 1 904886 14 0   £8.95

SELECTED POEMS Tassos Denegris. Translated into English by Philip Ramp. A generous selection of the work of a Greek poet with an international reputation.
ISBN 1 899549 45 9   £6.95

WHO Alan Dent. ISBN 1 904886 07 8   £8.95

THE OGLING OF LADY LUCK Alan Dixon. ISBN 1 904886 12 4   £8.95

THE NEW GIRLS Sue Dymoke. ISBN 1 904886 00 0   £7.95

COLLECTED POEMS Ian Fletcher. With Introduction by Peter Porter. Fletcher's work is that of "a virtuoso", as Porter remarks, a poet in love with "the voluptuousness of language" who is also a master technician. ISBN 1 899549 22 6   £8.95

LAUGHTER FROM THE HIVE Kate Foley. ISBN 1 904886 01 9   £7.95

OMM SETY John Greening. ISBN 1 899549 51 X   £5.95

THE HOME KEY John Greening. ISBN 1 899549 92 7   £8.95

LONG SHADOWS: POEMS 1937–2002 JC Hall. ISBN 1 899549 26 9   £8.95

A PLACE APART Stuart Henson. ISBN 1 899549 95 1   £7.95

CRAEFT: POEMS FROM THE ANGLO-SAXON Translated and with Introduction and notes by Graham Holderness. *Poetry Book Society Recommendation.*
ISBN 1 899549 67 6   £7.50

ODES Andreas Kalvos. Translated into English by George Dandoulakis. The first English version of the work of a poet who is in some respects the equal of his contemporary, Greece's national poet, Solomos. ISBN 1 899549 21 8   £9.95

FIRST DOG Nikos Kavvadias. Translated into English by Simon Darragh
ISBN 1 899549 73 0   £7.95

MR IRRESISTIBLE Angela Kirby. ISBN 1 904886 19 1   £8.95

A COLD SPELL Angela Leighton. ISBN 1 899549 40 4   £6.95

PAGING DOCTOR JAZZ: A Verse Anthology, compiled by John Lucas.
ISBN 1 904886 08 6   £10.00

THE OUTSIDER Christine McNeill. ISBN 1 904886 15 9   £8.95

ELSEWHERE Michael Murphy. ISBN 1 899549 87 0   £7.95

TOUCHING DOWN IN UTOPIA: POEMS Hubert Moore.
ISBN 1 899549 68 4   £6.95 Second Printing

MORRIS PAPERS: POEMS Arnold Rattenbury. Includes 5 colour illustrations of Morris's wallpaper designs. ISBN 1 899549 03 X   £4.95

MR DICK'S KITE Arnold Rattenbury. ISBN 1 904886 13 2   £10.00

MAKING SENSE Nigel Pickard. ISBN 1 899549 94 3   £6.00

THE ISLANDERS: POEMS Andrew Sant. ISBN 1 899549 72 2   £7.50

BEHIND THE LINES Vernon Scannell. ISBN 1 904886 02 7   £8.95

MEDAL FOR MALAYA: a novel by David Tipton. ISBN 1899549 75 7   £7.95

PARADISE OF EXILES: a novel by David Tipton. ISBN 1899549 34 X   £6.99

STONELAND HARVEST: NEW AND SELECTED POEMS Dimitris Tsaloumas. This generous selection brings together poems from all periods of Tsaloumas's life and makes available for the first time to a UK readership the work of this major Greek-Australian poet. ISBN 1 8995549 35 8   £8.00

TAKE FIVE 05: poems by Catherine Byron, John Lucas, Clare MacDonald Shaw, Peter Porter and Gregory Woods. ISBN 1 904886 17 5   £8.95

For full catalogue write to:
Shoestring Press
19 Devonshire Avenue
Beeston, Nottingham, NG9 1BS UK
or visit us on www.shoestringpress.co.uk